Ma'khai's Many Moods

Young Buddha Press

Ma'khai's Many Moods by Kasheera Hickson and Mark Savage Jr.
Published by Young Buddha Press Los Angeles, Ca 91405

www.YoungBuddhaPress.com

Printed in the United States of America

First Printing, 2018

For information about special discounts available for bulk purchases, sales promotions, fund-raising and educational needs, contact Young Buddha Press Company Sales at 1-707-276-6334 or info@youngbuddhapress.com.

Library of Congress Control Number: 2018903360

ISBN: 978-0-9990678-0-2

10 9 8 7 6 5 4 3 2 1

Dedicated to our beautiful son
Ma'khai. You are truly a bright light!

Happy

When your heart smiles, let it shine bright.

Curious

Asking questions is how we grow and explore the world.

Sad

It's okay to feel sad, tears help our hearts heal.

SHY

Sometimes shy is just the beginning of brave.

Excited

We jump for joy when we feel excited!

ANGRY

Anger is just your body saying, 'Something's not right.' It's okay to listen.

SLEEPY

Rest is powerful. Even superheroes need naps.

SURPRISED

Surprise is how your heart says, 'Whoa! Something new!

Frustrated

ven when it's tough, you're still learning. Take a break before trying again.

BORED

Boredom is your brain asking for something new to discover.

Worried

It's okay to feel unsure. You can ask for help.

SILLY

Can you make a silly face?

SCARED

Courage is feeling fear and showing up anyway.

LOVED

THE BEST FEELING IN THE WORLD!

www.ingramcontent.com/pod-product-compliance
Lightning Source LLC
Chambersburg PA
CBHW040252100426
42811CB00011B/1236